For Mum and Dad, thank you for giving me the world – CP

To Oscar, for your boundless curiosity, and Willow, for your radiant spirit – MA

A catalogue record for this book is available from the National Library of Australia

ISBN: 9781486319855 (hbk)
ISBN: 9781486319862 (epdf)
ISBN: 9781486319879 (epub)

Published by:
CSIRO Publishing
36 Gardiner Road, Clayton VIC 3168
Private Bag 10, Clayton South VIC 3169
Australia

Telephone: +61 3 9545 8400
Email: publishing.sales@csiro.au
Website: www.publish.csiro.au
Sign up to our email alerts: publish.csiro.au/earlyalert

Edited by Dr Kath Kovac
Cover, text design and layout by Cath Pirret Design
Printed in China by Toppan Leefung Printing Limited

CSIRO acknowledges the Traditional Owners of the lands that we live and work on and pays its respect to Elders past and present. CSIRO recognises that Aboriginal and Torres Strait Islander peoples in Australia and other Indigenous peoples around the world have made and will continue to make extraordinary contributions to all aspects of life including culture, economy and science. The use of Western science in this publication should not be interpreted as diminishing the knowledge of plants, animals and environment from Indigenous ecological knowledge systems.

Note for readers: A glossary can be found at the back of the book.

Note for teachers: Teacher notes are available at: https://www.publish.csiro.au/book/8210/#forteachers

Aug25_01

THE WORLD FROM HERE

CASSY POLIMENI

ILLUSTRATED BY
MEL ARMSTRONG

PUBLISHING

Do you like to lie on your back
and look for shapes in the clouds?

Milo can see a band of gorillas
and a shiver of sharks.
What can you see?

The tendency to see faces, patterns or animals in nature and objects is called pareidolia (PAH-rah-DOLE-ee-ah).

Do you ever wonder what it would be like to reach out and touch a puff of cloud?

Would it feel like cotton wool? Or fairy floss?

The study of clouds is called nephology, and scientists who study clouds are called nephologists.

Clouds are a mass of tiny water droplets or particles of ice, or a mixture of both. They form when a parcel of air becomes so saturated it can no longer hold water in vapour form, so it turns into liquid droplets or solid ice crystals. When clouds form at ground level, we call them fog.

Maya watches the world below through the plane window.

Above the clouds, the sky is always blue.

Earth is not the only planet that has clouds. Mars also has clouds made from water, while the clouds on Jupiter are made from a gas called ammonia.

Things look different from up here, with Earth spread out below like a giant quilt.

Farm fields are usually rectangular. This makes them easier to plough, plant, water and harvest.

Each continent is divided into countries.
Do you recognise any familiar shapes?

More than 300 million years ago, all the countries of the world fit together like pieces of a giant puzzle. Known as Pangea, this ancient supercontinent was surrounded by a vast ocean called Panthalassa. Around 200 million years ago, when dinosaurs of the Jurassic period roamed Earth, Pangea began to break apart to form the continents as we know them today. And they are still moving – at a rate of just a few centimetres per year!
NORWAY
FINLAND
UK
EUROPE
ASIA
JAPAN
AFRICA
N
W
E
S
SOUTH AFRICA
AUSTRALIA
ANTARCTICA

Storm clouds roll across the sky, and Milo's mum calls him inside.

The plane begins to wobble. Maya feels like she is stuck inside a bowl of jelly, or sailing on a stormy sea.

Thunderstorm clouds are also called cumulonimbus clouds. They can produce thunder, hail and lightning.

Weather affects everything we do.

When the sky turns grey and rain pitter patters and thunder crashes and lightning flashes, it can be hard to see clearly. But that doesn't mean the things you love are no longer there.

You might have felt static electricity when you zoom down the slide at the park, or rub a balloon on your head until your hair stands on end. But did you know lightning is also static electricity? When frozen raindrops bump into each other inside a storm cloud, they create an electrical charge. When the charges connect with one another, this causes lightning.

If you're afraid, close your eyes. Take slow, deep breaths. Wait for the storm to pass.

When you feel scared, tune into your senses. Find a quiet space and notice:

- 5 things you can see
- 4 things you can touch
- 3 things you can hear
- 2 things you can smell
- 1 thing you can taste.

Things might look different after a storm, so pay attention.

Frogs love damp, humid conditions and are most active and noisy after rain. Wet weather provides them with perfect conditions to breed, feed, drink or move around.

Mushrooms often pop up after rain, and quickly produce microscopic seed-like spores. Wind and rain carry the spores into gardens, where they can turn into full-sized mushrooms within a day.

Go slow.

Notice the tiny details.

And don't forget to breathe.

Did you know that trees have their own 'fingerprints'? Tree rings tell the story of the weather during each year of the tree's life. Wide rings are a record of a rainy year with plenty of growth, while narrow rings show the year was one of dryness or drought.

Wonder is all around.

After a busy day, it can be hard to quieten your mind.

Some people count sheep to help them fall asleep. You could try counting stars!

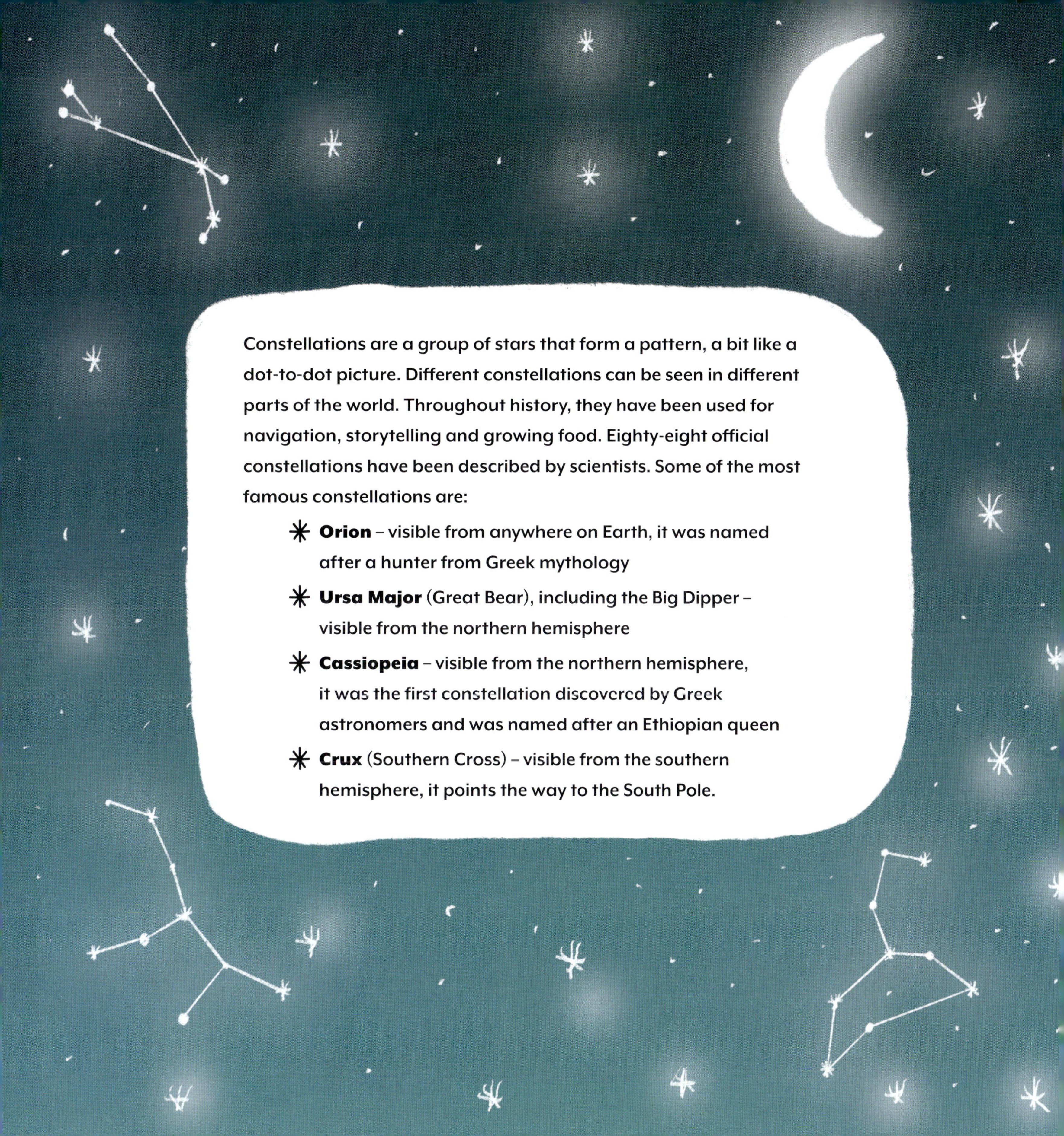

Constellations are a group of stars that form a pattern, a bit like a dot-to-dot picture. Different constellations can be seen in different parts of the world. Throughout history, they have been used for navigation, storytelling and growing food. Eighty-eight official constellations have been described by scientists. Some of the most famous constellations are:

- **Orion** – visible from anywhere on Earth, it was named after a hunter from Greek mythology
- **Ursa Major** (Great Bear), including the Big Dipper – visible from the northern hemisphere
- **Cassiopeia** – visible from the northern hemisphere, it was the first constellation discovered by Greek astronomers and was named after an Ethiopian queen
- **Crux** (Southern Cross) – visible from the southern hemisphere, it points the way to the South Pole.

When it's time to
face the world again,
keep your eyes open.

You never know
what's around the corner.

SCHOOL

Each day brings a
new world to explore.

FACTS ABOUT THE WEATHER (AND HOW IT MAKES US FEEL)

A matter of perspective

No one experiences the world like you do. The way we see things depends on where we are from, our beliefs and experiences, and even our mood.

At the beginning of this book, Milo and Maya are seeing the world from different places. Milo is looking up at the clouds and Maya is looking down from a plane. This is called physical perspective, and refers to what you can see or sense from where your body is in physical space. But Milo and Maya also think and feel differently. This is called emotional perspective.

The way you experience the world is one of the things that makes you special. Realising others might experience things differently, and trying to listen and understand their perspective, is what makes a good friend.

What is weather?

Weather is the way that the atmosphere feels to us at a particular time and place. It can include sunshine, rain, snow, wind, fog and hail. Weather changes depending on the season, and which part of the world you live in. It can also vary according to the shape of the land and how much sunlight it receives, how far the land is above sea level and how close it is to the ocean. The weather can even vary within a small area. Have you ever noticed that it might be raining where you live, but not on the other side of town?

Types of clouds

A cloud's height, shape, colour and the surrounding weather tell us what type of cloud it is. Cloud names come from Latin – for example, cirrus means a curl or lock of hair, while cumulus means a heap. Scientists group clouds into 10 main types, which are divided into 27 subtypes. The 10 main types of clouds are:

- cirrus
- cumulus
- stratus
- altocumulus
- altostratus
- cirrocumulus
- cirrostratus
- cumulonimbus
- nimbostratus
- stratocumulus.

Lightning, thunder and hail

Lightning is a supercharged form of static electricity – the same energy that makes your hair stand on end when you go down a slide at the park. When frozen raindrops bump into each other inside a thundercloud, they create an electrical charge. After some time, the entire cloud fills with electrical charges that can be negative, positive or neutral. The positive and negative charges are attracted to one another. When they connect, they form lightning.

Lightning heats the surrounding air to temperatures of 30,000 degrees Celsius. That's around five times hotter than the Sun! The heat causes the air to expand in a fraction of a second. The rapid expansion of air squeezes the air in front of it. This creates a shock wave, causing the crashing sound we know as thunder. Because light travels faster than sound, we see lightning before we hear thunder.

When raindrops are carried upwards on warm, moist air during a thunderstorm into extremely cold areas of the atmosphere, they freeze and form hailstones.

Wild weather

Hurricanes, cyclones and typhoons are all names given to giant, spiralling, tropical storms that form over water, and have high winds of at least 119 kilometres per hour. The name depends on where the storm develops. If it forms over the North Atlantic, central or eastern North Pacific oceans, it is called a hurricane. Over the South Pacific and Indian oceans, it is known as a cyclone, and in the north-west Pacific it is called a typhoon.

Tornadoes form over land. These narrow, rapidly rotating columns of air extend from a thunderstorm to the ground. Other examples of wild weather include heat bursts, dust storms called haboobs, and tornadoes of water called waterspouts.

Morning Glory clouds are the world's most spectacular example of a roll or volutus cloud. These rare, tubular cloud formations can be 1,000 kilometres long and move at speeds of 60 kilometres per hour. They have been spotted around the world, but can only be reliably predicted over the outback town of Burketown, Queensland, where they appear from late September to early November each year.

Hector is the name given to a thundercloud cluster that forms almost every afternoon at 3 o'clock over the Tiwi Islands in Australia's Northern Territory between September and December. Named by World War II pilots and ship navigators, Hector can reach a height of 20 kilometres. That's around the cruising height of a commercial aeroplane! Hector's reliability makes it a perfect subject for meteorologists (scientists who study the weather).

How weather affects us

Humans, other animals and plants are all affected by the weather. If it rains too much or not enough, or if it is too hot, cold or windy, it can affect our health and even our mood. Do you sometimes feel uneasy before a storm? That might be your body sensing a drop in atmospheric pressure. Our energy levels might go up or down depending on the temperature or the amount of sunlight. Some people feel tired or sad when it has been raining for a long time, while pluviophiles love it!

Weather affects us all in different ways. But one thing is true for all of us: time spent in nature is proven to make us happier and calmer, and helps us worry less. Green is good!

GLOSSARY

Ammonia (ah-MOWN-ee-ah): a chemical made up of nitrogen and hydrogen that smells nasty!

Atmosphere: a layer of gases that surrounds planets, including Earth.

Cirrus (SIH-russ) clouds: delicate and feathery clouds, mostly made of ice crystals, which appear high in the sky. They are the fastest-moving cloud.

Continent: very large land masses surrounded by oceans or seas. There are seven continents on Earth – Africa, Asia, Australia, Europe, North America, South America and Antarctica.

Cumulonimbus (KEW-mue-low-NIM-bus) clouds: huge clouds that form on hot days, when hot air full of water vapour rises upwards. They can result in heavy rain and hail.

Cumulus (KEW-mue-luss) clouds: large, white, puffy clouds that form when the air is warmed and rises. They sit low in the sky and are often seen on sunny days.

Drought (DROWT): a long period of no rain and very dry weather that can last for months or years.

Hemisphere: half of Earth, either side of the equator. Australia is in the southern hemisphere. When it is summer in the southern hemisphere, it is winter in the northern hemisphere, and vice versa.

Lenticular (len-TIK-yu-lar) clouds: clouds shaped like almonds – or flying saucers!

Microscopic: unable to be seen without a microscope.

Pluviophile (PLOO-vee-oh-file): someone who loves rain and rainy days, and particularly the sound of rain.

Season: one of several cycles of changing conditions in the environment throughout a year.

Spores: the seed-like structures that fungi, such as mushrooms, use to reproduce.

Stratus (STRAH-tuss) clouds: low clouds that look like thin, white sheets and often form in valleys and hollows.

Water vapour: the transparent (see-through) gas form of water.